Practical Business Communication

Practical Business Communication

TIM J. SABEN

Business Skills Express Series

McGraw-Hill

New York   San Francisco   Washington, D.C.   Auckland   Bogota   Caracas
Lisbon   London   Madrid   Mexico City   Milan   Montreal   New Delhi
San Juan   Singapore   Sydney   Tokyo   Toronto

McGraw-Hill

A Division of The McGraw-Hill Companies

This publication is designed to provide accurate and
authoritative information in regard to the subject matter
covered. It is sold with the understanding that neither the
author or the publisher is engaged in rendering legal, accounting,
or other professional service. If legal advice or other expert
assistance is required, the services of a competent
professional person should be sought.

*From a Declaration of Principles jointly adopted by a Committee
of the American Bar Association and a Committee of Publishers.*

Library of Congress Cataloging-in-Publication Data

Saben, Tim J.
   Practical business communication / Tim J. Saben.
     p.   cm.—(Business skills express series)
   ISBN 0-7863-0227-5
   1. Business communication.   2. Business writing.   I. Title.
II. Series
  HF5718.S22   1994
  651.7—dc20   93–33173

Printed in the United States of America
5 6 7 8 9 10 ML 0 9 8 7 6 5 4 3 2 1

PREFACE

The growing mountain of information and the speed with which it swarms around the globe means that there is fierce competition for your readers' time. Consider, for example, the following:

- Annually some 346,000 tons of newsprint are used for the *New York Times*.
- About 3,600 tons of ink are used. This could give each resident of Wichita, Kansas two gallons a week for one year.
- New information generated in the last 30 years was greater than the amount produced in the previous 5,000 years.[1]

Practical Business Communication is designed to be useful whether you have years of business writing experience or if today is your first day at work. Also, the book is useful for refresher seminars and as a reference guide.

Information overload, which produces anxiety, will not go away. However, writing is not as difficult as most of us insist on making it. If you can organize your ideas verbally, you can also write them down in an interesting way.

Unfortunately, too many writers approach their business messages fearfully or routinely. The result is that words sound self-important or boring. Either way the message dies.

As a business writer, it is vital that you ask these six questions:

1. Who is my audience?
2. What can I do to make my messages clear, even enjoyable, to read?

---

[1] R. Wurman, *Information Anxiety* (New York: Doubleday, 1989), pp. 33, 35.

3. When do I want to obtain results?
4. Where does my reader work, live, and play?
5. Why am I writing the message?
6. How can I help my reader?

Practical Business Communication will answer these questions and give you answers to many others. Good luck!

Tim J. Saben

ABOUT THE AUTHOR

Tim J. Saben holds a Doctorate of Education from the University of Oregon and has taught in high schools, community colleges, and universities in Australia, Canada, England, Kenya, and the United States. Currently, he teaches business communications at Portland Community College, Portland, Oregon and conducts business writing workshops and seminars for personnel in sales, production, and community services.

About the Business Skills Express Series

This expanding series of authoritative, concise, and fast-paced books delivers high-quality training on key business topics at a remarkably affordable cost. The series will help managers, supervisors, and frontline personnel in organizations of all sizes and types hone their business skills while enhancing job performance and career satisfaction.

Business Skills Express books are ideal for employee seminars, independent self-study, on-the-job training, and classroom-based instruction. Express books are also convenient-to-use references at work.

CONTENTS

Self-Assessment

Writing memos and letters is a challenging, rewarding, and increasingly important responsibility. Check your approach to business writing by answering the following statements.

	Almost Always	Sometimes	Almost Never
1. I think about my reader before I write.	_____	_____	_____
2. I realize that my reader's time is more important than mine.	_____	_____	_____
3. I know that initially, the medium is more important than the message.	_____	_____	_____
4. I organize my message around one main idea.	_____	_____	_____
5. I avoid abstractions and provide details.	_____	_____	_____
6. I use words to express—not impress.	_____	_____	_____
7. I often use present tense and parallel structure, and avoid doublespeak.	_____	_____	_____
8. I remember the difference between denotation, connotation, and tone.	_____	_____	_____
9. I include reader benefits and obtain feedback from the reader.	_____	_____	_____
10. I avoid fallacies.	_____	_____	_____
11. I am firmly reasonable in saying no.	_____	_____	_____
12. I proofread messages for errors and legal problems.	_____	_____	_____
13. I don't make assumptions about foreign readers.	_____	_____	_____
14. I don't use group- and gender-biased words.	_____	_____	_____

1 | The Communication Process

This chapter will help you to:

- Think about the audience before you write.
- Use Who? What? When? Where? Why? How?
- Understand the interaction of medium and message.
- Employ Maslow's theory to give your messages a human face.
- Use good writing manners.

Recently, on a flight from St. Louis, Missouri to Portland, Oregon, the pilot's intercom shattered the nicotine–free gloom of the smokers and the restless sleep of nappers.

The captain said, ''This is your captain speaking. We do not have enough fuel to reach Portland. When we land at Sioux City we hope to take on more fuel, which will take about an hour. Thank you.''

Some passengers interpreted those words to mean, ''This plane is probably going to crash. Good-bye.''

Unfortunately, the airline pilot did not think about what he wanted to communicate. He only thought about what he wanted to say, and he assumed that his listeners knew almost as much as he did. Hearing his own voice only served to reinforce the idea that he had been clearly understood. After all, he had heard what he had said.

If he had recognized that his passengers needed both information and knowledge, he could have said:

"This is your captain speaking. This plane is probably going to crash."

Good evening ladies and gentlemen. We are encountering 90–mile–an–hour headwinds. This wind and our full load means that we are using more fuel than usual. Consequently, we are diverting to Sioux City, North Dakota, to top up the fuel tanks as a safety precaution. Refueling in Sioux City will take about one hour. I apologize for the unavoidable delay. Thank you. ∎

CONSIDER THE AUDIENCE

Before you even begin to approach your audience, try and see your complete message from your listener's point of view. If you do, there's a better chance that your audience may read what you have written, or listen to what you say. If you ignore your audience, they won't read or listen to your messages and unfortunately, you probably will not know this. Consequently, you may continue to churn out unread, ineffective letters, memos, and reports forever.

Communication in the 1990s is overwhelming. There is more information, using many different forms of media, being aimed at greater numbers of people segmented into increasingly diverse groups. Consequently, the better you know your readers, the more effective your persuasive appeals will be. You need to develop both a specific focus (or insight) and the external worldview (or oversight) for your messages to come across to any audience.

QUESTIONS TO ASK

When you're ready to communicate (out loud or in writing) ask:

Who is your primary and secondary audience?

What activities do they prefer and what benefits or rewards can you give them for reading your message?

When will the message be received and when could they provide the time or money to become involved?

Where does your audience live and where do they go on vacation?

Why send your message and why should your message appeal to them?

How can you get interest and obtain feedback from your readers?

How does the writer of the following memo ignore the audience?

TO: All ABC employees
FROM: Vice President, Plant Services, Judy Green
DATE: 4/14/93
SUBJECT: Smoking Policy

I must tell all employees again about our nosmoking policy. Open flames and careless smoking are becoming a danger to all of you in the building. This has got to stop. We are working with increasing amounts of flammable materials. This fact makes it even more important that you all follow the policy.

Signs will be posted to tell you about restricted areas. They should clearly define restricted and nonrestricted areas. You are to follow the signs.

There will be two mandatory meetings on Tuesday. I will listen to your ideas and I will explain disciplinary action for violators. There will also be a special guest.

Day and night crews: See your supervisors for meeting times. Office workers: Please attend the one that best fits your schedule.

■ Exercise 1.1

Take a few minutes to think about how the writer ignored her audience. How would you react?

1. What basic errors does the writer make about the audience?

_____

_____

_____

_____

2. How would you react to this memo if you were an employee at ABC Corporation?

_____

_____

_____

_____

3. Rewrite the memo as if you were Judy Green.

TO:

FROM:

DATE:

SUBJECT:

_____

_____

_____

_____

_____

_____

_____

_____

_____

_____

_____

_____

_____

_____

_____

DREAMS VS. REALITY

To understand the flaws of Judy Green's memo look at the first diagram on page 5. Ms. Green probably had this simple vision of her message being sent to readers.

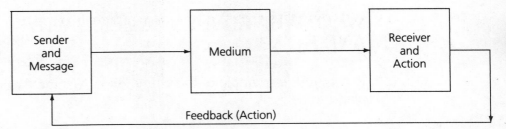

THE DREAM

Judy Green made the fundamental mistake of assuming that her readers would read what she had written while ignoring other message obstacles. Her assumption did not recognize the reality of communication theory, as shown below.

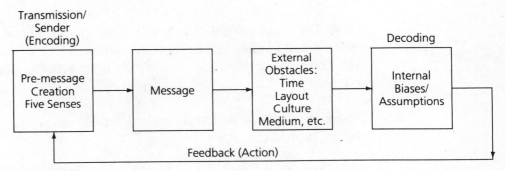

THE REALITY

Most written messages encounter some, if not all, of the obstacles in The Reality boxes above.

1. Do you think about the audience before composing your message?
2. Have you thought about the ways that the message will be received?
3. Have you considered external obstacles, such as the day and the time that your message will be received?
4. Are you aware of internal biases and assumptions held by your readers?
5. Have you made it easy for the reader to stay in the communications loop? Have you included a phone number; allowed for a question and answer period?

You can avoid these pitfalls by asking the six crucial questions that follow.

WHO? WHAT? WHEN? WHERE? WHY? AND HOW?

Return to the example of the airline pilot. Assume that you are flying the plane.

You could have rapidly scanned your mental communications panel, just as you were checking the gauges, lights, and switches in the cockpit. Then you could have asked yourself six questions.

Who Is the Audience?   Probably a cross section of people. Definitely tired, since there had been many delayed flights out of St. Louis because of snow. You know that many of them may not like to fly.

What Did You Want to Say?   The plane would be making an unscheduled landing as strong head winds and a full load were eating up fuel. The only problem lay in the one hour refueling time. For this you apologize.

Where Would You Be Landing the Plane?   Sioux City, North Dakota or Sioux City, Iowa?

When Would the Plane Land?   You could also have told your passengers the miles and flying time to Sioux City, North Dakota. This information could have helped calm any nagging thoughts that the plane was actually running out of fuel.

WHEN and HOW are already covered.

With this information the passengers could return to their flight secure in the knowledge that the skies were not only friendly, but also safe.

THE MEDIUM AND THE MESSAGE

Once you've overcome listening obstacles by asking the questions who?, what?, when?, where?, why? and how?, you need to pay attention to the mode, or medium of message transaction.

We get information through our five senses: touch, sight, taste, hearing, and smell. Consequently, the form the information takes becomes the medium that transmits information—in many cases the medium actually *is* the message.

These media can be objects that you can actually touch, such as a computer keyboard; that you can see, a television program for example; that you can taste, such as ice cream; that you can hear, such as a train whistle or a song; or that you can smell, like dusty streets recently washed by rain.

But many memos and letters in business communications contain messages that act independently from the content of those memos and letters.

For example, what do the following words instantly bring to mind?

1. Business communications.
2. Memos.
3. Letters.
4. E-mail.
5. Fax.
6. CD-ROM.

These words may have different meanings for each of you, since before you actually read a memo, you have usually formed an opinion about the message. The result is often that you may pay scant attention to the contents. The medium has become the message.

Sensory Overload

Some media have been so overused and their messages often predictable that readers tend to ignore their content altogether. Consequently, many messages are ignored.

Many pieces of direct mail, for example, do not survive the short walk from the mailbox to the front door. For a medium that accounts for approximately $21 billion a year, this inability to retain the readers' attention is serious. When you open your mailbox, you may be happy to see mail there, but the initial feel of the postcard-size mailer tells you that the message is of no consequence because it feels light. Then you notice something like the "code" shown on page 8.

*CAR-RT SORT**8127**
D2-5155
THE RESIDENT
16586 WISH WAY
ABILENE, TX 79604

> The senses of sight and touch help people decide on the value of the medium. What independent information do the senses of touch and sight communicate to you before you even read the card?
>
> **1.** Touch.
>
> _____
>
> _____
>
> **2.** Sight.
>
> _____
>
> _____

In addition, your sense of belonging is insulted if you have lived at that address for at least two or three months. If someone wants to write to you, you may reason, they should at least know your name. *The resident* is rather like yelling, "Hey! You!" In addition, you also know that the back of the mailer will probably contain coupons for pizza, carpet or drape cleaning, or muffler and shock absorber replacements.

Types of Media

We're accustomed to getting most of our messages through the familiar media listed below.

1. Print media: newspapers, magazines, memos, letters.
2. Electronic media: radio, television, E-mail, fax.
3. Film media including video tape recorders.
4. Recorded music: records, cassette tapes, compact discs.
5. Transportable visuals: billboards, trade fairs, conventions, T-shirts and sweatshirts, and street graffiti.

As you are probably well aware, *these* are the media that will get messages to an audience. Recognize their power and influence!

MASLOW'S THEORY AND BETTER COMMUNICATION

In 1936, Dr. Abraham Maslow described a hierarchy of needs that act as motivations to human behavior. This hierarchy is shown below.

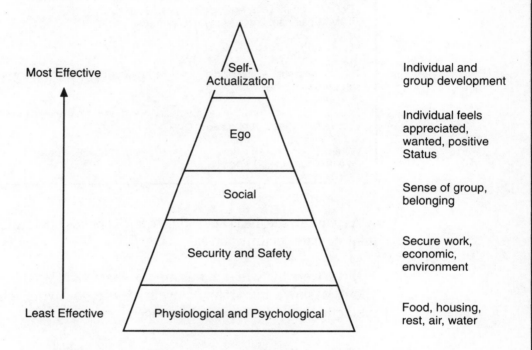

SUPERVISORY CATEGORIES from LEAST EFFECTIVE to MOST EFFECTIVE

Once lower level needs are met, people are motivated to reach toward the next level.

Maslow and Common Sense

How does Maslow's theory relate to communication? Let's look at an example that illustrates the resuls of *ignoring* an audience's needs.

TO: All employees, ABC Corp
FROM: Chairman, Entertainment Committee
DATE: 8/8/92
RE: Annual Company Picnic

The annual picnic will be held at Oak's Park, August 14. Management will provide coffee, soft drinks, and hot dogs.

Due to security reasons, we cannot guarantee theft from vehicles and unattended tables. Consequently, do not bring any valuables.

We are looking for an enjoyable time as members of ABC Corporation. So be there. Sign up with your supervisor today!

As you can see, he is appealing to social needs but is not attending to the intermediate security and safety needs.

If you were the writer of this memo what would you have written? Think about Maslow's hierarchy of needs before you write. Then, rewrite the memo in the space provided on page 11.

■ **Exercise 1.2**

TO:
FROM:
DATE:
SUBJECT:

_____
_____
_____
_____
_____
_____
_____
_____
_____
_____
_____
_____
_____
_____
_____
_____
_____
_____
_____

BE YOURSELF

In your daily interactions with others, you use pleasant words and a positive tone because you know that aggressive and negative words usually result in resistance. What, then, do you regard as the three most courteous words.

1. _____

2. _____

3. _____

Most people know "what is right" in their written dealings with others and know what constitutes good manners.

1

However, due to stress and problems, many people let bad manners creep into their writing.

A BAD MANNERS MEMO

TO: All CRM employees
FROM: Regional Supervisor, Bill Bonnetti
DATE: December 22, 1992
SUBJECT: Theft

We will no longer have any type of honor snack system, as we have AGAIN proved that we could not handle this type of responsibility.

The first box of cookies and candy came out to be $20.00 short, and the second box proved to be $42.20 short. I have compensated the snack company out of my own pocket because I feel strongly that this theft is a poor reflection on CRM employees. I was brought up to believe that such actions constitute theft—plain and simple theft.

So once again, a few bad apples have spoiled it for everyone.

Happy Holidays.

Bonnetti sounds as if he regards all CRM employees as thieves. Then he congratulates himself for paying the missing $62.20. Finally, his Happy Holidays appears to be sarcastic.

■ Exercise 1.3

Take a minute to turn bad manners into good ones. How would you
rephrase the CRM memo?

TO:
FROM:
DATE:
SUBJECT:

_____
_____
_____
_____
_____
_____
_____
_____
_____
_____
_____
_____

As you can see, practical business communication is built on a solid
foundation of understanding your audience's perception of messages,
needs, and motivators as filtered through sensory and written media.

Chapter 1 Checkpoints

✓ Think of your readers in terms of their Who? What? When? Where? Why? How?

✓ Identify the best type of medium for your message.

✓ Select positive, personable words that appeal to the reader.

✓ Use good writing manners.

2 | Organize and Clarify Your Writing

This chapter will help you to:

- Write with a purpose.
- Wear the reader's shoes.
- Avoid abstractions, give details.
- Present one main idea.
- Organize your message.
- Use words to express—not impress.

Bill Headrick made a sales call in the small town of Kenworth, and on returning to his car he noticed a parking ticket on the windshield. He was irritated because he hadn't noticed a No Parking sign. Now he saw a faded painted sign on the road.

That evening Bill wrote a letter to the Kenworth Town Hall clerk protesting the ticket because of the barely visible sign. A week later he received a reply.

Mr. Headrick,

There was an error in the amount you owe for citation no. 14564 to Kenworth for your parking violation.

Your ticket shows that you owe $18, but only $14 is really owed. Due to your letter, the judge suspended $14 from $38 and wrote $28 as your fine, but we will count the lower amount.

Thank you.

Colleen

Bill read and reread the letter. Did he owe $18, $14, or $28? There was no tele-phone number on Colleen's note, so he would have to call information, because the town was not listed in his directory. ■

Exercise 2.1   Your Reaction?

If you were in Bill's shoes what would you do? Would you call Colleen? Mail a check for one of those three amounts? Write directly to the judge, enclosing the letter from Colleen, asking for clarification? Do nothing?

_____

_____

_____

WRITE WITH A PURPOSE

It is impossible to calculate how many unnecessary messages are written in a day. Often a phone call or a few words spoken over coffee or in the parking lot could accomplish more than a written message. Too many peo-ple, like Colleen, send messages routinely without any clear purpose. Such messages are often written for an audience of one: the writer. Apart from irritating the reader, messages are also expensive to send; the time spent writing most memos and letters costs between $7 and $12.

If you ask yourself the question "Why write the message?", you will often find that a more appropriate medium (a phone call, a few words in passing, etc.) can be more effective and will save both time and money.

WEAR THE READER'S SHOES

Before you write a message, put on your audience's shoes, sit in their chairs, and try to imagine how your message will be perceived. Would you want to receive what you've written? Does your memo or letter look appealing? How long is it? Can the main idea be grasped quickly?

Consider the following example from a human resources director whose company was involved in individual departmental self-evaluation. All 230 employees received a one-paragraph memo form after the evaluation.

TO: ALL EMPLOYEES
FROM: HUMAN RESOURCES
DATE: SEPT. 1, 1993
SUBJECT: EVALUATION

Assessment of progress to date has been hampered by an uneven level of understanding concerning our current project that is being inculcated into the Company's projected objectives and feasible procedures aimed at increasing market share. In the fullness of time, however, all employees will understand the overall architectonic process.

Exercise 2.2

How would you react to the memo on page 17?

1. _____

2. _____

3. _____

4. _____

5. _____

6. _____

The four steps listed in this chapter will help you write clear and direct memos.

1. AVOID ABSTRACTIONS

Abstractions are open to interpretation by the reader and can sometimes cause confusion. Abstractions weave their way through your messages, creating fog banks of confusion.

For example, if you ask someone to define *happiness* you will probably get something like this: "feeling good," "being safe," "content," and so forth. Then, if you ask someone to define any of those phrases, the reply will probably be: "Feeling happy." You still do not know what they mean by the term *happiness*.

If, however, the person who you first asked replied, "Feeling good about learning how to water ski, driving a car, or write a well-written memo," you will know exactly what that person means by happiness.

Provide Mental Pictures of Your Message

Concrete verbs, nouns, and details and examples give your readers a series of mental pictures. These pictures let your readers see your meaning. When you write, you are like an artist painting a picture. The words you use become the images and the colors that help the reader understand exactly what you mean. Clear wording gets rid of abstractions.

If you are having difficulty writing a message, it may be useful to circle the words (usually verbs and nouns) that convey a picture. Should you find that there are only one or two circled words, your message is probably too abstract.

Review and Practice

Reread the human resources director's memo. Now write a clearer version of what the director tried to communicate.

_____

_____

_____

_____

_____

_____

_____

_____

_____

2. PRESENT ONE MAIN IDEA

Imagine that the main idea you want to communicate is a tree, and the trunk is the main point. Connected to the trunk are the branches, twigs, and leaves. The same can be said of your written messages. The chosen medium, the first appearance of the content, and the length of sentences and paragraphs all contribute to the overall effectiveness of that trunk, or main point.

If something detracts from the main idea, prune it off!

Before You Write

Before you start writing, write a sentence that clearly states the one main point of the memo or letter. Another helpful device is to draw a picture (even using stick figures) of your main point. If you cannot write that sentence or draw the picture, then you probably do not have a clear idea of what you want to communicate.

2

3. ORGANIZE YOUR MESSAGE

When organizing your message, pay attention to your audience and the form the appeal takes. Generally, there are two main ways to approach your readers:

1. Indirect/informal.
2. Direct /formal.

Regardless of the approach, you must take into account the message's main point. If the content is very serious or demands immediate action, the direct plan is usually more effective. However, your common sense and good manners will be the ultimate judge of which approach you should take.

The following indirect/informal memo appeals for donations to the Cystic Fibrosis Fund. The writer is a secretary at a large law firm. She began by asking herself the six questions described in Chapter 1:

Who?—a senior partner in a law firm, who is an avid golfer.

What?—donation toward the CFF.

When?—Tuesday, August 18, 1994.

Where?—Lake Obegon Country Club.

Why?—funds for continued research for CFF.

How?—golf tournament.

INDIRECT/INFORMAL MEMO APPEALING FOR DONATIONS TO THE CYSTIC FIBROSIS FUND

Mark Twain once described golf as "a good walk—ruined."

I don't know much about golf, and I suspect that Twain knew even less, but I know that you do. Consequently, I am inviting you to participate in the Cystic Fibrosis golf tournament:

DATE & TIME:　　　　Tuesday, August 18, 10 AM
LOCATION:　　　　　Lake Obegon Country Club,
　　　　　　　　　　Barnes Road (218) 786-9991
TOURNAMENT DUES: $75

You once told me that as a teenager you overcame severe speech problems. In certain ways my best friend, Heather, mirrors your tenacity. She has cystic fibrosis, and she was not expected to live past the age of 15. Last December she celebrated her 21st birthday. She is a full-time college student and works for the Cystic Fibrosis Foundation.

This year's CFF golf tournament will be most enjoyable. The teams are organized around a foursome. Should you be willing to participate, I could find three other attorneys from those already signed up to accompany you.

Although Mark Twain will be unable to participate, would you be interested? If you are, please call me at ext. 234 by Thursday, June 13.

Thank you.

Steps in the Indirect or Informal Approach

1. Write a short, attention-getting opening paragraph. If you know or are acquainted with the reader, then you can use the type of approach used by the CFF writer.

If you do not know the reader, begin with a reference to some unusual event that occurred recently that the reader must have noticed. Such a reference could include a particularly prolonged hot spell, unusual water rationing, an earthquake, or the success of a sport team playing in national finals.

2. Get to the point in the second paragraph. Be sure to make a smooth transition to that paragraph. The writer of the CFF appeal cleverly used Twain as the transition device.

3. If necessary, provide more information or details in the next paragraph.

4. In the last paragraph, make a statement or ask a question. In this section you should try to obtain physical or mental reaction from the reader. Depending on the persuasive memo or letter, provide a channel for the reader to contact you: a telephone or fax number, a room number, a questionnaire to be completed, or a self-addressed stamped envelope (SASE).

■ Hint ─────────────────

Note

If you have difficulty in closing, you may return to your first paragraph and select a person, place, or an idea to neatly tie up the message. The CFF writer, for example, mentions Twain again.

■ Hint ─────────────────

Caution

A common form of starting indirect messages is to begin with a question. This approach, however, is not advisable unless you know the reader well, since we have been conditioned to answer questions without much thought. Try turning to someone and asking the time, the date, or how to get to 43rd and Vine. Most people will answer. But if you open a memo or letter with "Are you interested in forming a health group?", "Can you come to a meeting on the budget?", many readers will answer the easiest way: no. Your subsequent message crashes before it can fly.

The following memo was attached to a copier machine in a 30–person office whose members had worked together amicably for at least eight years. The machine was malfunctioning, and the secretary was being interrupted at least 10 times a day to fix it.

DIRECT/FORMAL MEMO ABOUT A MALFUNCTIONING COPIER

TO: You Copyists
FROM: The Copy Machine
RE: WARMING UP, RUNNING ME

You are not getting your copies printed, because you are ignoring my "feel good" spot. It is marked with a yellow sticky adhered to my front door.

If you press firmly on that spot and continue to apply pressure, I will print for you. If you don't . . . forget it.

Thank you.

Steps in the Direct or Formal Approach

1. State the main point in the opening paragraph. Do not bury the point so that it is unclear.

2. Expand on the main point by using reasons why your message should be considered. The message must present information that is in the reader's best interest. This approach may take more than one or two paragraphs, depending on the main point. If numbers or figures are used, you may wish to consider changing the layout to make that information clear.

3. Follow the same path for closing as with the indirect/informal approach.

■ Exercise 2.3

Select three areas involving time, money, or both in your work or home environment that you would like to see changed. List them below.

1. _____

2. _____

3. _____

Write the opening paragraph asking for change for two of the three areas. One paragraph could use the indirect approach, and the other one could use the direct approach.

1.

_____

_____

_____

_____

2.

_____

_____

_____

_____

4. USE WORDS TO EXPRESS—NOT IMPRESS

Sometimes when people write, they may have a tendency to use phrases that sound educated, or use longer words, thinking that they are more impressive.

Words, however, are like bank accounts—they can be squandered easily. Do not use words that are inappropriate for the intended audience. Avoid using words that are not a part of your daily vocabulary. Don't attempt to impress the reader; it destroys your tone and will bore your audience.

Five Suggestions

The writer George Orwell offered excellent advice on this subject. He suggested that writers should never:

1. Use an expression that is a cliché.
2. Use long words in place of short words.
3. Be wordy.
4. Use the past tense when the present is acceptable.
5. Use foreign phrases, technical words, or jargon if English phrases and words are applicable.

■ Review and Practice

Rewrite the following sentences keeping the five suggestions in mind:

1. Although it has been raining cats and dogs lately, do not leave wet umbrellas in the Customer Reception area.

   _____

   _____

2. In case of inclement weather, call your supervisor.

   _____

   _____

3. I realize that some employees, wherever you are in the building, will be unable to attend the Safety Meeting.

_____

_____

4. The Safety Committee appreciated your comments.

_____

_____

5. We are striving to project the ambiance of la belle Paris in our sales letters.

_____

_____

Chapter 2 Checkpoints

✓ Always write with a clear purpose.

✓ Imagine that you are the reader.

✓ Use picture words, give details, and avoid abstractions.

✓ Organize your message around one main idea.

✓ Use words to communicate your message, not impress the reader.

3 | Plan for Readability

This chapter will help you to:

- Get attention by using layout or appearance.
- Avoid five main common errors.
- Use present tense, parallel structure, and avoid doublespeak.
- Emphasize and de-emphasize ideas.
- Be real.

GET ATTENTION

The First Paragraph

No one will understand your message unless the message is quickly accessible, appealing to the eyes, well thought out, and "real." This chapter will help you get and keep your reader's attention.

Your opening paragraph should get your reader's attention and establish your sincerity. In keeping with other types of memos and letters, make that first paragraph short: two to three sentences. Don't use more than 27 words for the longest sentence.

Use Visual Devices

In a world that is relying more and more on the visual aspects of communication, use of visual devices in memos and letters is on the rise. In the last 10–15 years, highway signs and daily newspapers have turned to pictures. For instance, the "Merge Left" and "Freeway Ends" warnings are being replaced with visual representations of these phrases. Similarly, the daily

"Do I really have to read all this?"

newspapers are using front-page symbols to give readers a rapid view of the weather: rainy, cloudy, hot.

Though pictures may quickly project a thousand words, they can also destroy the message if they are overdone. Use the following cautions when using visuals:

- Use pictorial aids sparingly, or they clutter up the message with visual noise.
- Use moderation in the size of the visual, or it appears that you are shouting at the reader.
- Use visuals only if they are clear and of good quality.
- Use visuals that are appropriate for the audience.
- Use visuals to compliment—not dominate—the message.
- Use of visuals will probably increase your printing costs.

An easy way to educate yourself about the use of visual aids is to notice what attracts you. Your mailbox is a marvelous self-teaching tool. Also, listen to the types of advertisements that pop up in conversation and those that the media "talk" about. Why do your friends like or dislike them? What do they remember about the ads?

Avoid Layout Problems

The message will probably not be read if:

1. Your words are surrounded by too much visual noise or clutter.
2. There is not enough white space.
3. The sentences and paragraphs are too long.
4. There are too many numbers within the paragraphs.

Consider the following memo and letter examples illustrating the four types of errors.

THE MEMO: Version 1

TO: Camille Blixby
FROM: Marcia Klovisky
DATE: October 29,1992
RE: SAIF Audit

I received a phone call today from a SAIF auditor, Karlie Smithe, to set up a time that would be convenient to audit our payroll records for FY 91(7/89–6/90). She will be here at 8:30 on November 8.

She will be investigating our quarterly reports for the fiscal year 1990, our earnings records for FY 90, our SAIF payments for FY 90, and examining whether or not people were paid within the right category for FY 90. Her identification number is KLS6539802.

THE LETTER: Version 1

ABC Computers, Inc.
Sales Division
34 Bedford Way
Chicago, IL 76812

February 6, 1993

Ms. G. Gledover, President
MarHill Manufacturing
9832 Belmont Drive
Chicago, IL 60606

Dear Ms. Gledover:

Although you had mentioned last week when I met with you that you wish to keep your current computer system and improve on it by adding new software, I would like to offer an alternative that I think you will find attractive. Two weeks ago, ABC Computers announced a new computer system that permits companies of your size a true multisize, multitasking environment for a reasonable price. ABC calls it our High Task System 93. It is not only a state of the art computer, but it also has a wide selection of software available to run on it. Given the chance to peruse your interest needs, I am confident that the System 93 will work well in your business environment and that we can find an excellent software solution for your specific needs.

Because we have not appraised your specific needs, I cannot offer what I feel is the best solution. However, I do think that we might be able to offer a solution, once identified, for around $30,000. If this is true, based on qualifications, we can tie that amount into an ABC Credit Lease Option for around $900 per month for five years. This is only $321 more per month than you are currently paying for data processing. If this were broken down into an hourly rate, based on a 40-hour week, your cost is only $3.07 per hour—a small investment considering that it will increase your data processing capabilities up to a level your company expects and deserves.

This letter is written in the clear knowledge that you are not now looking for a computer. However, there are a few things to consider when looking at your data processing needs and what it takes to achieve those needs. If you would like to sit down and visit, in more detail, about what ABC has to offer, please give me a call.

Sincerely,

Sheila Sims

■ Review and Practice

Take a minute or two and review the list of layout problems. Then write down your reactions to both the memo and the letter. How would you fix them?

1. _____

   _____

2. _____

   _____

3. _____

   _____

4. _____

   _____

Both these examples show how easy it is to destroy messages before they are actually read. The following memo and letter show how layout errors *can* be avoid.

THE MEMO: Version 2

TO: Camille Blixby
FROM: Marcia Klovisky
DATE: October 29, 1992
RE: SAIF AUDIT FISCAL YEAR 1990

The SAIF auditor, Karlie Smithe, will be auditing Petro's payroll records for fiscal year 1990: June 1989 to June 31, 1990. She will be here at 8:30 AM on Tuesday, November 8.

The FY 90 areas to be reviewed are:

- Quarterly reports.
- Earning records.
- SAIF payment records.
- Correct payment personal categories.

Karlie's identification number is KLS 6539802.

THE LETTER: Version 2

Dear Ms. Gledover:

Thank you for the time that you spent with me last week. I enjoyed the visit very much.

You said that you would be keeping your present computer system but that you would update it by purchasing new software. I would like to offer you, however, an alternative for your consideration.

For $3.07 an hour ABC Computers could offer you a new computer system that offers companies your size multiuser/task capabilities. I am confident that ABC's High Task 93 provides superior solutions for your needs. For example, I feel—following a more thorough evaluation of your business requirements—that the HT 93 could provide you with the following major advantages:

- Quality products and local service.
- Superior software solutions.
- ABC Credit Lease options.

If I can be of help in identifying your requirements, and ABC's solutions, in greater detail, please call me at (503)111-3124.

Sincerely,

Sheila Sims

FIVE WRITING ERRORS TO AVOID

The following five main errors in business communications invite your readers to stare out of the window, refill their coffee cups, go to the bathroom, or do almost anything rather than continue reading.

1. *Sentences that are too long.* If sentences are between 40 and 60 words in length, it is because the writer is unclear about the main purpose. The result is that sentences often contain two or three main points. If possible try to keep sentence length to 27 words or less.

2. *Too much preamble.* The writer uses too many introductory phrases and conditional clauses before getting to the subject of the sentence.

3. *No image.* Too many words contain no image for the reader to "see," and he files such information in the black hole of memory.

4. *Passive distant language.* Too many sentences are impersonal in tone and use the past tense.

5. *No variety.* Too many sentences begin with "I" or "the."

■ Review and Practice

Rewrite the following sentences avoiding the errors just described.

1. Considering the present information and recognizing the importance of those figures in the present business climate that seems to be improving slowly, an upturn in the company's market should happen.

   _____

   _____

   _____

2. Our company offers you advice on empowering yourself and others so you can fulfill visions of greatness in which leadership is a mastery of the process of leading.

   _____

   _____

3. Payroll wanted to tell you that changes in deductions cannot be made between pay periods, as this has caused too many problems in the past.

   _____

   _____

4. I will keep you updated on the project. I plan to include some departmental meetings to do this. I look forward to your input at those times.

   _____

   _____

OTHER ISSUES

Present Tense

Where possible, write your messages in the present tense. This verb form gives life and immediacy to your sentences. Obviously, your use of past, present, or future tense is dictated by time, events, and so forth.

Remember that many readers do not pay much attention to grammar. They do possess, however, an internal ear, which is quick to recognize the past tense as conveying information that is past history. That historical filter encourages the reader to ignore your message or, at least, file it as something that can wait.

Present Tense Examples

1. If you're wondering how far we'll go to win you over, please continue reading. We are including an attractive financial plan that will show you how sincere we are.

2. I am enclosing two quotations for the Jalasol 26. One copy is for Tom Haelpine.

Past Tense Examples

1. Have you ever wondered how far we went to win you over? If so, we have included an enhanced financial plan that was designed for you.

2. Two quotations have been included for the Panasol 26. As you requested, I included a quote for Tom Haelpine too.

Hint

Note:

A rough guide is to use verbs ending in *-ing* and avoid verbs ending in *-ed*.

Parallel Structure

There is a lot of confusion over the term *parallel structure*. This is probably caused by the word *structure*, which sends many of us reeling back to junior high school grammar classes.

Think in terms of how to present information so that, like railroad lines, each category is parallel to its neighbor and looks as if it is constructed in the same way. If you choose a verb to open a sentence, follow this pattern. Similarly, if you start your sentence with a noun, continue using nouns for following sentences.

A very common error is using unparallel structure when listing. The following lists show parallel structure within each list. Note how the left list items begin with present tense verbs, and all items in the right list begin with nouns followed by past tense verbs.

Presenting information.	Information presented.
Providing materials.	Materials provided.
Informing participants.	Participants informed.
Offering feedback.	Feedback offered.
Collecting questionnaires.	Questionnaires collected.

The next examples show the confusion that may arise from mixing verbs, nouns, and tenses.

Presenting information	(verb, present tense, noun).
Materials provided	(noun, past tense verb).
Participants informed	(noun, past tense verb).
Offering feedback	(verb, present tense, noun).
Collecting questionnaires	(verb, present tense, noun).

 Exercise 3.1

Make the numbered terms below parallel.

Please follow the procedures below for ordering supplies:

1. Place your order as soon as possible.
2. Ticket order forms must be filled out correctly.
3. Orders cannot be processed over the telephone.
4. Ordering supplies can only be done through this department.
5. There will be no refunds.
6. If you had any questions, please call.

3

1. _____

2. _____

3. _____

4. _____

5. _____

6. _____

Avoid Doublespeak

Doublespeak is using words to confuse or deliberately mislead an audience. William Lutz, author of *Doublespeak*,[1] identifies four types of this disease:

   1. *Euphemisms*. Words are used to present offensive information as acceptable. For example: "downsizing" for reducing; "reduction in force" for layoffs; "payola" for bribe.

   2. *Jargon*. The language of specialization that confuses the layperson. For example: "The students' evaluative criteria will be based on the stochastic process." (Translation: Student tests will be based on random variables.)

   3. *Gobbledygook/bureaucratese*. Long words and sentences are used when short ones are available. For example: "The conceptualization process interfacing with ABC's objectives will be prioritized in empowering input interactive small symposium environments." (Translation: ABC's objectives will be discussed in small groups that will list those objectives in order of importance.)

   4. *Inflation*. The simple is made complex. For example: "We at ABC cannot, should not, will not allow our differences to become obstacles in providing services to our diverse constituency. Thus, the national motto: 'E Pluribus Unum.' " (Translation: Cultural differences at ABC should be a source of strength.)

   A short stroll around your home may reveal such examples as: "Total empowering control coordinator" for a desk diary; "The Mark QXV1

---

[1] W. Lutz, *Doublespeak* (New York: Harper Perennial, 1990), pp. 2–6.

advantage" for a computer disk; "Eco-Logically H20 conservationalism without compromise" for a water-saving toilet device; "The ultimate unequalled total synchronistic audio system" for a CD speaker. You get the point.

EMPHASIS

An additional way to clarify your message and keep your reader's attention is by choosing to highlight items or to detract attention from them.

You can emphasize your ideas in the following ways:

1. Use a simple sentence (subject, verb, object).
2. Use the idea as the subject of the sentence.
3. Use action/picture-producing verbs and nouns.
4. Use the imperative mood (a command or request).
5. Use a list (1, 2, 3) or bullets.
6. Use a statement that says the idea is important.
7. Use a one-sentence paragraph.
8. Use a well-known comparison if the idea may be obscure. For example, change "The product measures $3\frac{1}{2}$ by $4\frac{1}{2}$" to "The product is about the size of a TV remote control."
9. Use repetition for longer memos and letters.

In some cases, you will want to downplay less important aspects of a letter or memo.

You can de-emphasize your ideas by:

1. Using the passive voice.
2. Using the subjunctive voice.
3. Using a dependent clause.
4. Using the idea in the middle of a sentence or paragraph.

Review and Practice

Try to emphasize different ideas by writing single-sentence examples on page 38.

3

1. _____

2. _____

3. _____

4. _____

5. _____

6. _____

De-emphasize the six ideas you wrote in the sentences above.

1. _____

2. _____

3. _____

4. _____

5. _____

6. _____

BE REAL

Reader Perception and Readability

In print, credibility is far harder to obtain than in a face-to-face meeting, because the reader cannot see your facial gestures or body language. Consequently, it is important to be aware of how your message may be perceived by the reader.

If the source of the message is not seen as believable by the audience, the message will be seen as unbelievable. In such cases, no matter how deft the sentences, the message will be cast aside or, at least, will encounter resistance.

Avoid Fallacies

Fallacies are errors in logic that may sink your message by destroying the reasons and logic behind your sentences. They are nearly always inferential or active. Avoid the following fallacies, if possible:

1. Misplaced cause and effect. The writer assumes that one event causes another. For example, walking under a ladder and then getting fired or eating eggs and getting high cholesterol.

2. Either/or reasoning in which the writer assumes that there are only two extremes. For examples, either you are happy or sad, or you are fat or thin.

3. Bandwagon. This fallacy assumes that everyone is doing something, so the reader better do the same. For example, everyone's going to the meeting or all the other employees like the idea.

4. Authority or the well-known person. A well-known baseball star advertises a brand of coffeemaker. Therefore, that brand must be superior and do what he says it does.

5. Ad hominem (a cocktail circuit term for "attacking the speaker"). This fallacy smears the character or abilities of people. For example, he's a police officer and he drinks, the CEO doesn't know anything, and she's too old.

6. Half-truths/propaganda. The writer twists the truth by providing only half the information or by taking comments out of context.

7. Generalizations/oversimplification. The writer assumes that people, events, and so forth, fall into all-encompassing categories. For example, all teenagers use drugs, or unions are opposed to management.

■ Practice and Review

Write an example for each of the seven fallacies.

1. _____

_____

2. _____

_____

3. _____

_____

4. _____

_____

5. _____

_____

6. _____

_____

7. _____

_____

Chapter 3 Checkpoints

✓ Get attention with the layout/appearance.

✓ Avoid five main written errors.

✓ Use present tense, parallel information, and avoid doublespeak.

✓ Emphasize and de-emphasize ideas where appropriate.

✓ Avoid false logic, or fallacies, in your writing.

4 | Writing Style and Presentation

This chapter will help you to:

- Write a "read me" opening paragraph.
- Understand denotation, connotation, and tone.
- Recognize the symbolism of language.
- Include reader benefits.
- Provide feedback opportunities.
- Proofread.

GETTING READY

Too often you approach business writing wearing your "interview clothes." You place yourself in an adversarial role: them and me. You fall victim to your fears. Your initial attitude dooms memos and letters. In this regard, writing is like many things that you do. Take bowling. If you approach that first roll of the ball with resentment, loathing, or anxiety, you are better off staying home, because a negative attitude keeps you from doing your best. The same thing is true for writing business communications. You are the only one who can change that attitude.

Writing effective letters and memos is a challenging, creative, and often a satisfying activity. Relax. Take off your shoes. Think. Plan. Write.

"READ ME" PARAGRAPHS

The four major flaws in weak opening paragraphs are:

1. Paragraphs are too long and intimidating.
2. Sentences are longer than 27 words.

4

3. There are too many main ideas.

4. The paragraphs are boring because they are too vague.

PUT YOUR FIRST PARAGRAPH ON A DIET

If possible, try not to use more than 3 to 5 lines in your first paragraph. If you can get readers to complete that first paragraph, the chances are they will stay with you. After all, how many magazine and newspaper articles, books, and even films have you read or watched precisely because you started them and had already invested time in them?

Most readers, however, will not even bother to read those opening lines if you use the baseball-bat approach. This style ignores the importance of the medium, visually slams the readers' corneas, and gives the following message: "What follows is boring and a waste of your time. Do not read it."

AN OVERWEIGHT PARAGRAPH

TO: Flor Fernandes, support services supervisor
FROM: Al Jones
DATE: May 12,1995
REGARDING: PROBLEMS WITH THE COPIER IN ACCOUNTING OFFICE

The accounting staff is experiencing continual jamming problems with the copier. The problems occur many times each day. As an example, time sheets are copied on ivory paper. It is almost impossible to copy eight sheets without at least one jam in the attempt. White paper also causes considerable problems but not as consistently. Please help us by determining if the copier is causing the jamming problem and then have it repaired, or, if the quality of the paper is the culprit, help us to solve that problem.

It is difficult to track the work time lost due to copier problems, but it is considerable.

Abcdefg hijk Lmnop. Qrstuvwxyz abcdefg Hijkl mnop abcdefg Hijkl mnop Lmnop. Abcdefg hijklmnopqrstu Vwxyz. Ab Cdef ghij klmnop qrst uvwxyz. Abcd ef Abcdefg hijk Lmnop. Qrstuvwxyz abcdefg Hijkl efg Hijkl mnop Lmnop. Abcdefg hijklmnopqr z. Ab Cdef ghij klmnop qrst uvwxyz.

efg Hijkl mnop Lmnop. Abcdefg hijklmno xyz. Ab Cdef ghij klmnop qrst uvwxyz. Abc Qrstuvwxyz ab mnop. Abcdefg Ab C ghij klmnop q Abcd ef ghij Lmnop. Hijkl mnop Lmnop. hijklmnopqrstu Vwxyz. Ab Cdef ghij klm st uvwxyz. Abcd Efg hijklm no.

That same memo is more effective if presented in the following form.

THE SLIMMER PARAGRAPH

TO: Flor Fernandes, support service supervisor
FROM: Al Jones
DATE: May 12, 1993
RE: COPIER PROBLEMS, ACCOUNTING OFFICE

The accounting staff needs your help, as their copier is continually jamming.

For example, copying eight time sheets on ivory paper causes jamming. White paper also jams, although not as often.

Work time lost to copier problems is difficult to assess. It is, however, considerable. Consequently, would you please help us to determine if:

1. The copier needs repairing?

2. The paper quality is the culprit?

Please contact Alan, Rm. 23, or call ext. 157 with advice/suggestions.

Thank you.

Exercise 4.1

Rewrite the following so that the first paragraph is clear and no longer than three lines.

Jim, as per our conversation of this afternoon when we talked about the JHG number that is for the sole purpose of tracking and routing JHG contract numbers while the JHG is in JHG status only. Once a contract has been let and a contract number assigned, the contract number and only the contract number will be used to identify the contract.

_____

_____

_____

_____

_____

_____

_____

Use 5- to 27-Word Sentences

Most memos and letters arrive with a built-in disadvantage. That is, their physical form immediately tells the reader that the memos are not really important, and they can be ignored, usually without much penalty.

Consequently, if you keep the opening sentences from 5 to 27 words, you can help put the first paragraph on a diet. Also, you will add to the readers' positive approach to your later messages.

Sentences from 5 to 27 words are usually clearer and more concise than longer sentences. You have probably only launched one main idea in that paragraph.

BE CREATIVE

Dare to fail. Be creative. Don't be boring. This is much easier with an audience you know well. You can, for example, use appropriate humor. You could refer to a person, place, or thing that would be instantly recognizable.

If you do not know the readers well, you could rely on a number of sources to provoke interest. For example, what information do you have about the reader? Is it her birthday? Has she been promoted or just returned from a vacation?

Use Quotes

The following memo opener was written to a group of computer salespeople inviting them to attend a day seminar on business writing.

Memo Opener

"When I use a word," said Humpty Dumpty, "It means just what I mean it to be. Neither more, nor less."

Unfortunately, many in Humpty's audience ignored him. They didn't understand what he meant to say.

If you find yourself in such situations from time to time, I would like to invite you to a business writing seminar . . .

In the openers, quotes were used to get attention and appeal to audience characteristics. Notice that the quote is "softer" and probably engaging. If you were writing to a different group, you would need to choose a different quote to suit the mood.

Don't Antagonize!

Beware of the audience; it is very easy to antagonize or confuse your reader. Try to involve the reader positively. Be sure to avoid mixed messages by following the guidelines on denotation, connotation, and overall tone.

DENOTATION, CONNOTATION, AND TONE

Writing style relies on these related characteristics that channel the meaning of language. These characteristics are denotation, connotation, and tone.

Denotation

Denotation is the dictionary definition of a word. *Connotation*, on the other hand, is what a word implies, or whose meaning is generally accepted.

As you realize, English is a remarkably adaptable and innovative language. For example, a teenager may use the word *outrageous* in a negative way while describing to her parents the low grade she received on a school report. Later, she could use the same word in a positive sense to describe the soccer skills of a friend.

Further, the same denotation can mean many different things to both receiver and sender. For example, take the word *cool*. If you look it up in the dictionary, you'll find something like this:

cool (kool) adjective, moderately cold; neither warm nor very cold.

But we all know that cool can also be defined, or denoted, as hip and stylish.

Connotation

In written communication, words change their meanings in context and thus have various connotations. Consequently, two speakers can have the following conversation:

"What's the trouble with my engine? The car starts but then dies."
"That's cool. Maybe . . ."
"Cool? No it fires up and then dies."
"Like I said, it's cool. Chill out. It's OK."

After the fuel problem has been fixed, the "cool dimensions" form a different connotation.

"Here's the bill. I know it's not cool, but it is Sunday."

Bewildering? Of course. This same confusion can appear in your letters and memos when you ignore the connotation of words; this usually happens when you do not know your audience. In this context, it is interesting to realize that in English the word *set* has 194 different meanings! One hundred twenty-six are verbs, 58 are nouns, and 10 are adjectives.[3]

Tone

Tone is the cumulative effect of the words you use in your memos and letters. Tone is the attitude that you convey about your message and an unconscious mirror of how you regard your audience.

Exercise 4.2

What do you see as the connotation associated with the following memo subject headings?

1. MANDATORY MEETING (to clerical workers in a medium firm).

_____

_____

2. SLOPPY EATING AND DRINKING (to all employees, large firm).

_____

_____

3. TOWING YOUR CAR (to all employees, small firm).

_____

_____

---

[3] S. Ober, *Contemporary Business Communications* (Boston, MA: Houghton Mifflin, 1992), p. 29.

THE SYMBOLISM OF LANGUAGE

As you are aware, a symbol stands for something else. Symbols can be divided into two groups: those that have a limited meaning, and those that have an accepted meaning due to years of public use. For example, knowledge of your nickname or the reason you named the family dog are limited to a fairly small group. A national flag and an anthem are more widely understood, so they are public symbols.

Consider two points about symbolic language:

1. Be aware of the medium used and that the location of the symbolic language affects the intention behind the word or phrase.
2. Be aware of the audience.

The Medium and the Location

If you hear someone talking on the radio (medium and location), you will probably be more forgiving of grammatical lapses, presentation of material, and so on. Readers are less forgiving of these lapses in memos and letters.

Similarly, "The Clock's Tickin' in the Hood" would not be an effective editorial heading in the majority of newspapers although they might accept this in the sports section.

> ### Hint
> When you use a RE: or SUBJECT: in a memo or letter you use symbolic language. This is because the connotation of RE: or SUBJECT: calls attention to the heading and the subsequent message. Imagine, for example, receiving a memo beginning RE: The Clock's Tickin' in the Hood about layoffs!

The Importance of Audience

Symbols contain different meanings for different groups. For example, when Governor Bill Clinton appeared on "The Arsenio Hall Show" and played the saxophone, he helped to change the symbol of a presidential candidate and, hence, the perception of some voters. The differences between President George Bush and Governor Clinton were dramatically illustrated.

READER BENEFITS

Beyond language, style and a good opening, you need to make your readers *want* to read your memo. What's in it for them?

1. Use the "you" approach to involve readers.
2. Give your readers tangible benefits of reading your memo or letter such as price reductions, good service, and availability.
3. Provide ways for your readers to become physically involved in the communication process.

Benefits can be tangible and intangible. Intangible benefits are those that the reader can *sense*, such as good tone, appropriate connotation, and the right audience appeal. In addition, offer the following real benefits.

The Most Common Tangible Benefits

1. Visual

The layout of the memo or letter.

The typeface and font size used.

The length of the message (one-page persuasive messages are usually the most effective).

The presence or absence of color.

The inclusion of a telephone/fax number, SASE (a self-addressed stamped envelope), and so forth.

2. Tactile

The feel of the paper (higher quality bonds are more desirable, especially for letters).

The weight or number of pages of the message, especially for reports.

The SASE.

USE THE "YOU" APPROACH

Write to the readers as if you were speaking to them personally. For example, "You are invited to attend a meeting on Departmental Budget Expenditure" is more effective than "I am inviting you to attend a meeting on Departmental Budget Expenditure."

Exercise 4.3

Use the "you" approach with the following sentences, so they do not start with "I."

1. I am urging all employees, if possible, to car pool.

_____

2. I am writing to introduce myself as your county relief officer.

_____

3. I want to thank you for the time you spent with me.

_____

4. I think we can expand our Ft. Worth-Dallas area market share.

_____

Exercise 4.4

There are times (serious complaint letters, etc.) when you may wish to start with "I." Give three examples of the types of memos and letters that you would start with "I."

1. _____ **2.** _____ **3.** _____

Write three opening sentences for the types of memos and letters you selected.

1. _____

_____

2. _____

_____

3. _____

_____

PROVIDE FEEDBACK OPPORTUNITIES

As described earlier, you want to get the reader actively involved in communication.

1. Request the reader's involvement where appropriate.
2. Include a name and telephone number so you can be contacted if necessary.
3. Include a SASE or a "tear along the dotted line" card.

If you make it easy for the reader to become involved mentally, via layout and content, or physically, the reader becomes a willing participant in the message process.

PROOFREAD

Too many messages arrive with a built–in excuse to be ignored or even ridiculed. They are sloppily written with poor spelling, tortured logic, or elementary grammatical errors.

■ Exercise 4.5

Take a few minutes and think about what is wrong with the following sentences. Correct any mistakes you see.

1. Thank you for your letter. It's good to here from you.

_____

2. At ABC Corporation, it feels that a meeting is a good idea.

_____

3. Requesting your reply.

_____

One practical way of testing whether or not your message is grammatically correct is to read your memo or letter out loud. Your ear is a superb editor. Try it with this memo.

TO: Building Members
FROM: Department Chairperson
DATE: May 18, 1992
RE: THIEVES

We have had two incidents of theft—purses stolen from Alison Eik and a person in the Reception Center—as well as some vandalism in the last few days.

4

You may not be able to point out the exact grammatical problem here, but your ear will probably tell you that the phrase "purses stolen from Alison and a person in the Reception Center" is somehow wrong. Notice that it appears that Alison had a couple of purses stolen and that a person was also taken from the Reception center.

Hint

Caution

If you are using a computer, it is advisable to print a copy before you send the message. Many people think that because they wrote the message they know what has been written, so they scan the content. They do not read the material.

Review and Practice

Review Chapter 4 and rewrite the following memo that was sent to approximately 200 people.

TO: All Employees, C2 Building
FROM: Bill Welldon
DATE: 9/23/95
SUBJECT: Coffee Shop, C2 Building

Thank you for your expression of disappointment and interest in the company's food services. I am sorry that continued operation of the C2 coffee shop was not possible. As you know, food services is an auxiliary enterprise at ABC. It must be self-supporting and not look to the company's funds for any support. Toward that end, I look to the food service manager to monitor costs constantly and to recommend to me how we can provide service within available revenue.

Beth Washington, the food service manager, is working hard to get costs and income for the company's food services in line. The volume of business at the C2 coffee shop was inadequate to keep the services open.

However, Beth is making an effort to keep coffee services as close as possible (physically as well as fiscally) by opening a station in the H4 building. While the opening of the H4 service is not as convenient as having it in your own building, it won't be too far away and will be an enhanced offering, since there will be more types of pastries and coffees.

_____
_____
_____
_____
_____
_____

Chapter 4 Checkpoints

✓ Be yourself when you write.

✓ Write a "read me" opening paragraph.

✓ Remember that denotation, connotation, and tone can affect your message.

✓ Watch for words that contain symbols that appeal to different audiences in different ways.

✓ Include reader benefits to reward your readers.

✓ Provide feedback avenues so your readers become involved in your message.

✓ Proofread to avoid elementary mistakes that ruin your message.

5 Good News Messages

This chapter will help you to:

- Use attitude, information, and tone to make routine messages more interesting.
- Give reasons for sending good news and goodwill messages.
- Be brief and sincere in closing your message.

A supervisor was concerned that the memos and letters written by company employees were not proofread closely enough. Her concerns were about accuracy and company image. She wrote a memo to all employees on the subject of proofreading. Unfortunately, the employees' errors did not improve.

Consequently, the supervisor wrote a follow-up memo. She gave some examples of memos received by insurance companies from customers who were filing accident claims.

Coming home, I drove into the wrong house and collided with a tree I don't have.

I collided with a stationery truck coming the other way.

The guy was all over the road. I had to swerve a number of times before I hit him.

I had been driving for 40 years when I fell asleep at the wheel.

The indirect cause of this accident was a guy in a small car with a big mouth.

To her delight many employees spoke to her about her last memo, reviewed their own work more carefully, and wrote error-free memos. ■

MAKE ROUTINE MESSAGES MORE INTERESTING

As you can see in the previous scene, humor is a delicate instrument to use and often is successful when you know the audience well. It can be effective in making routine communication interesting.

■ **Exercise 5.1**

In what routine, good news, and goodwill situations would you use humor? What would you write? Give three examples of your opening sentence.

1. _____

_____

2. _____

_____

3. _____

_____

Routine, good news, and goodwill memos and letters are often difficult to write because they are routine. People tend to approach such memos and letters the same way they drive: automatically. As a result they adopt a ho-hum approach.

The Ho-Hum Approach

This ho-hum view is primarily due to three major causes: the writer's attitude, clarity of information, and tone of the letter or memo.

Attitude.   Due to a negative, get-it-over-with attitude, you may ignore both layout and word choice in your haste to complete the memo or letter. Consequently, your routine messages often omit important information, such as the time and place for a meeting or a relevant phone number.

Information.   The backbone of good news and goodwill messages is the information they contain. Your information, however is not understood until the reader translates it into knowledge.

The process of acquiring knowledge—vital for understanding or comprehension—starts with the reader accumulating information. It is *your* job to present enough information in a clear, organized manner so that the reader can unlock your meaning.

Your words go through a filter in which the reader's values are added or subtracted to your information. The filtering process depends on whether your language is static/passive or inferential/active.

Static/passive words.   Static/passive words are facts or fragments. They contain information only. There is no connotation and no knowledge. For example, the following phrase is gibberish. The reader can only guess what the blanks represent: "Sixty-nine per cent of 2,200 _____ in North Carolina _____ name a single African country south of the Sahara." The sentence is static/passive.

Active/inferential words.   Active/inferential words provide a bridge that permits information to be decoded into knowledge by the reader. Return to the example above. Add the words "students," and "'could not" to the blanks in that sentence. Now the reader turns the information into knowledge and draws conclusions.

▮ Exercise 5.2

Notice the difference in the following two sentences:

1. There will be a meeting at 2:30 in the Spruce Room.
2. The agenda for the budget meeting, at 2:30 PM in the Spruce Room, covers allowances for travel and expenses.

What active/inferential values do you attach to the second sentence? Why is that sentence more effective than the first?

_____

_____

_____

_____

5

Tone.   In this context, tone refers to the actual sound made by words, as opposed to the overall feeling of a memo as described in Chapter 4. Many nouns and verbs can be divided into two groups: soft sounding (euphonious) and harsh sounding (cacophonous). Euphonious words, which usually emphasize the vowel sounds, are often less picture provoking and have less of an immediate impact than cacophonous ones in which the consonants are dominant. Thus, words such as *good*, *courtesy*, and *praise* are less powerful than *destructive*, *sarcasm*, and *threat*.

■ Exercise 5.3

For a moment think about the different images produced by the following two sentences:

1. Mr. Paul Kavuma is leaving ABC on Tuesday, January 31.
2. Mr. Kavuma will be terminated at the end of the month.

What is the active/inferential word in the second sentence? Why does that word infer a negative tone about both Mr. Kavuma and the company's management?

_____
_____
_____
_____
_____

Fortunately, good news and euphonious words have an inherent advantage over bad news. Adlai Stevenson once said that, "Americans are suckers for good news." Unfortunately, not enough managers and supervisors are producing good news for employee consumption. Consequently, many routine, good news, and goodwill messages ignore attitude, information, and tone, and they are so routine that the positive effect of the good news is lost on the reader.

ASK SIX QUESTIONS AS YOU WRITE

As in all memo writing, ask six important questions: who?, what?, when?, where?, why?, and how? In routine, good news, and good will messages these six areas are often ignored.

Once you have asked the six questions, you'll have the basic information needed to set up your memo. Remember to put "TO:" first to acknowledge that the receiver is the most important element in the communications process. The "RE:" or "SUBJECT:" should clearly spell out the memo's main point.

Introduction

Use a short opening paragraph (no more than two sentences). Get immediately to the point by using the "you" approach. It may be possible to start with a brief "thank you."

If you know the reader well, you can begin with a reference to an area of mutual interest, the reader's hobby, or an event that is memorable or amusing. For example:

1. Thank you for the time and ideas you gave as a member of the Building Improvement Committee.
2. Your help in keeping the parking lot clean and litter free is greatly appreciated.
3. Please remember that your Health Benefits Plan MUST be signed by you before Tuesday, May 16.

Hint ───────────────────────────────

Note

Always include the day and the date in your memos. Many people recall a day for some future event or activity, but they do not remember the date. For example, most people who have a dental appointment next Wednesday or Thursday recall the day of the appointment, but they could not instantly tell you the date.

GIVE REASONS

Stating the reason for your memo is crucial. This knowledge makes those routine memos and letters appear less routine; for example, don't write only that there is a meeting but briefly state the agenda, too. In other words, don't be vague about the reason you are sending a memo in the first place. Vagueness is a sure signal to stop reading.

Main Body

In this section, provide additional information that helps give the reader knowledge.

Examples

1. The committee's suggestions and ideas are excellent. I was particularly impressed with two areas.

    a. The realistic cost analysis for meeting our Disabilities Act responsibilities.

    b. The request for providing on-site child care.

    The president will be considering those two concerns at the meeting with department heads on Monday, June 14.

2. The time and money spent on removing litter from the parking areas has been reduced by 20 percent or about $100 per month.

Closing

Be brief and sincere! Keep the concluding paragraph short. You can conclude in a number of ways depending on your knowledge of the reader and the main point of the message.

Examples

1. Again . . . thank you.

2. Your continuing help in removing litter is much appreciated.

3. If you need any forms or assistance, please see John, Rm. LL4 or call him at ext. 154.

■ Exercise 5.4

Using the guidelines presented in Chapters 1–4, try your hand at writing good news and goodwill letters based on the topics listed.

Good News

1. New facilities are being built that will decrease the current overcrowded conditions. Those facilities, however, will not be ready to be occupied for about four months during which time there will be an increase in noise and other nuisances.

2. A bakery will be supplying your grocery store daily with fresh-baked bread and pastries. Any baking requests will be considered.

Introduction

_____

_____

Main body

_____

_____

_____

_____

_____

_____

_____

Conclusion

_____

_____

Goodwill

1. An employee has gained a promotion and will be moving to
   another company located in the same town. That company is a
   competitor.
2. The owner of a paving company has received a letter from the state
   highway department congratulating the construction crew for their
   excellent work.

Introduction

_____

_____

_____

Main body

_____

_____

_____

_____

_____

_____

_____

_____

_____

Conclusion

_____

_____

_____

Chapter 5 Checkpoints

✓ Pay attention to the attitude, information, and tone of your memo.

✓ Get to the point in the first paragraph.

✓ Give reasons that explain why you sent the message.

✓ Be brief and sincere in closing.

CHAPTER

6 | Bad News Messages

This chapter will help you to:

- Retain goodwill while delivering bad news.
- Avoid clutter in your memos.
- Be firm and reasonable.

Bad news comes in three forms: mild, moderate, and severe. These messages should be honest, say no, and retain the reader's goodwill.

The indirect approach is best for mild and medium messages. You should use the direct approach and come to the point early with severe memos and letters. It's more forthright and less painful than tiptoeing around the issue.

RETAIN GOODWILL

1. Start with a short, positive introduction.
2. Present the information using clear data and examples, while avoiding negative lecturing tones.
3. State the refusal only once.
4. Use smooth paragraph transitions.
5. Give the reader tangible and intangible benefits if possible.
6. Allow the reader the time and channels with which to respond.
7. Close on a positive note.

AVOID CLUTTER

Don't announce bad news with a poorly laid out memo, which, in effect, says, "You won't like this, but go ahead and read it anyway."

If possible, use a short memo format for bad news memos. A long form often causes you to feel that you have to fill up the page. This results in wordy and unclear messages.

Emotional clutter in memos and letters is caused by inferential and active words that can be misinterpreted.

Phrase	Reader's Reaction
As you know . . .	So? Why tell me again?
It has come to my attention . . .	Uh, Oh. The boss voice speaking.
This letter is about/I am writing to you about . . .	Get on with it. Show me, don't tell.
A decision has been made. . .	Faceless, buck-passing manager.
At ABC, we . . .	Who? Manager-employee division.
I sincerely regret . . .	Sure you do.
Obviously . . .	Yes it is /I'm not that stupid.
We are not accusing anyone . . .	Yes you are. And it's me.
To that end . . .	What end?
Thank you in advance for your coopera-tion. . .	Don't presume.
We know how valuable your time/mon-ey is . . .	Oh, no, you don't. That's why you think I'll give it away.
ABC's policy . . .	Reasons? Don't hide behind policy.

Exercise 6.1

Give three examples of phrases you have read in memos that provoke negative reactions like the previous ones.

1. The phrase: _____
   Your comment: _____

2. The phrase: _____
   Your comment: _____

3. The phrase: _____
   Your comment: _____

USE A BUFFER

Open bad news memos with a brief introduction or buffer. This should be positive and clear. The following examples show how to *not* start mild and medium bad news messages.

1. We're asking you to get your readers to buy a textbook that's so fascinating that you will find it hard to put down.

The use of "textbook" in conjunction with "fascinating," "will," and "hard to put down" produces an unintentionally insincere tone that both you and your readers instantly recognize.

2. If you subscribe now, Tim, you can save 20 percent off our regular newsstand price!!! Think about it, Tim!!! Act NOW!!!

Using a person's first name when you have never even met them is unwise. You are assuming too much familiarity. The exclamation marks are an example of overkill in which using too many is rather like laughing at your own jokes. They draw attention to the device at the expense of the message.

Be positive in the opening paragraph. A better opening paragraph for the two examples above would be:

1. ABC publishing company is confident that the book *Business Communications for Tomorrow* will prove to be valuable for your students.
2. Mail the attached subscription form by Friday, July 23, 1993 and save $6.50 off the newsstand price of *ABC Week*.

Mild Bad News

Consider the following situation concerning mild bad news.

Lisa is a receptionist who works in a common meeting and dispersal point for 58 employees in three different offices. By prior arrangement, each office takes a turn paying for the delivery of two national and two local newspapers. A few employees from those offices are taking sections of the papers and not returning them. Employees and waiting customers are complaining. ■

Lisa was asked to write a memo to all employees in the building.

LISA'S MEMO

TO: You guys
FROM: Lisa
DATE: ?
RE: NEWSPAPERS, RECEPTION LOUNGE

Please . . . please . . . PLEASE. Your help in solving a problem would be greatly appreciated by all of us. And that includes our customers.

A few of us are taking parts of the newspapers out of the reception lounge. This means that people in the building complain to me. The customers not only complain, but they do so when I'm trying to answer the telephones.

Consequently, I cannot easily answer the phones so that some incoming calls may be delayed or "lost." Also, it is difficult to answer routine questions from callers when I am trying to tell someone that a newspaper section must be "misplaced."

Please. Leave ALL SECTIONS of the newspapers in the reception lounge.

Thank you.

When Lisa submitted her memo to her supervisor for approval, she lectured Lisa on the use of "appropriate dignity," and "respect for professionals" and prepared the following memo:

THE SUPERVISOR'S MEMO

TO: All personnel
FROM: Lisa Cody
DATE: March 10, 1994
SUBJECT: NEWSPAPERS

Four daily newspapers are purchased for this building. They are delivered daily, except Saturdays and Sundays when the premises are closed. The intention is to have those papers for the benefit of all building tenants and their customers. They will remain in the reception for all to use.

The problem is that some of you are taking those papers, or certain sections, out of the RL area, and not returning them. This will stop. RESPECT THE SUBSCRIPTION OF OTHERS AND DO NOT REMOVE PAPERS THAT DO NOT BELONG TO YOU.

This intra-office memo was composed and prepared in direct response to the increasing newspaper problem. Our intention is to clarify what belongs to whom and for what purposes and what does not. I hope that this will help take care of this problem once and for all.

■ Exercise 6.2

Compare Lisa's memo with her supervisor's memo. What differences do you see? Which memo would you like to receive? Why?

1.

_____

_____

2.

_____

_____

3.

_____

_____

6

BE FIRM AND REASONABLE

Even though you may feel the need to apologize in bad news memos, *don't*. Make up your mind to say no and provide clear, objective reasons for that decision. The following excerpts from bad news memos show this assertive, nonapologetic tone.

DENYING A CREDIT APPLICATION

> Your application for ABC's credit card cannot be processed at this time. The reasons for this decision are that ABC's credit policy requires the following:
>
> **1.** Six month's residency at the same address before applying.
>
> **2.** Four month's full-time employment before applying.

DENYING A CLAIM

> Thank you for your letter of Wednesday, July 8 about ConsolAir's claim for $ 2,213.23.
>
> On Monday, June 25, Consul Air's Claims Department asked that you support your claim with a photocopy of your original invoice. Unfortunately, that document has not been received by Consul Air's Claims Department.
>
> I cannot process your claim without that document. Consequently, I am forced to reject your claim in full. However, should you submit a copy of the original invoice, your claim will be reopened immediately.

Severe Bad News

Although the process for writing mild, medium, and severe bad news messages is similar, there are three additional rules for writing severe bad news memos and letters.

1. You may write a longer memo or letter because of the more complex reasons, solutions, and so forth.
2. You should use the direct/formal style. If you use a buffer, keep it very short.
3. You should remember that you are writing to a human being whose life may be affected by the content of your message.

Exercise 6.3

If you had to write a dismissal message what would you say? What would you like to read if you were to receive such a message? In the space provided on page 73, rewrite the opening for the following severe, bad news letter:

> SUBJECT: NOTIFICATION OF TERMINATION
>
> As you know, it is obvious that ABC today faces one of the most challenging periods in company history. Unprecedented competition, an unpredictable world economy, plus an unrelenting explosion of technology are some of these challenges. Changing business conditions affected by these challenges make this letter to you necessary.
>
> A decision has been made to eliminate or reduce certain functions and/or positions in our organization. Specifically, your position as senior software/hardware engineer is being terminated.

RE:

_____

_____

_____

_____

_____

_____

_____

_____

_____

_____

_____

_____

_____

_____

_____

_____

_____

6

Avoid Legal Pitfalls

We are a litigious society and nowhere is this more obvious than in the business environment. As a business communications writer you should be aware of guidelines about what you can and cannot legally write. Consult a lawyer or *Black's Law Dictionary* for definitions of slander, libel, fraud, and misrepresentation and know your company's guidelines on avoiding these and other traps in correspondence and day-to-day business transactions.

MORE BAD NEWS: COLLECTION LETTERS

At some point in your career, you may need to follow up on a past-due bill. Although this can be unpleasant, it's a necessary task to keep business moving. You have four main goals when you write collection letters:

1. To obtain payment or return of a product as quickly as possible.
2. To keep your customer's business and goodwill.
3. To be consistent in the timetable between each mailing.
4. To be aware of legal implications.

Successfully reaching those goals depends on how you present your message. Usually, you will follow these steps: inquiry, appeal, and ultimatum.

Step 1: The Inquiry, Reminder Letter

Your layout and the accompanying message should be brief, pleasant, and assume that the reader has honestly forgotten to pay. Avoid a tone that could destroy goodwill. Make it easy for your reader to pay by offering to help if necessary. Of course, your company may have specific guidelines on payment schedules.

It is always a good idea to include specific facts about the purchase, balance, and amount due. If you place the information in the letter, you won't have to make a copy of the account and include it with the letter.

SAMPLE INQUIRY LETTER

Company Letterhead
Address
Area code and fax, Phone number

February 10, 1993

Purchase:	$ 3,500
Item:	20,000 flyers
Payment:	$00
Amount Due:	$ 3,500

Reader's address

Dear Deanne Wilson,

At your request on January 10, 1993, ABC Graphics printed, sorted, and posted 20,000 flyers for your direct-mail campaign. We hope that campaign was successful.

This letter is simply to remind you that the amount you owe ABC Graphics is $3,500. I'm sure that you have just forgotten to pay and that the payment is coming. If you are having any difficulties, however, please contact me so that I can be of assistance.

If you have already sent your payment, please disregard this notice with our thanks.

Sincerely,

COLLECT CALLS ACCEPTED.

Step 2: The Urgent Appeal Letter

This letter should be direct, but you can still be helpful. Do not ask your reader questions about the product or service. Avoid a moralizing or lecturing tone. Your approach with the urgent appeal message can be more flexible with customers who have a good credit history.

Drop the "Dear" and use a colon in the salutation. Do not use contractions, such as *we've*, *you'll*, *I'll* in your message. They are less formal and urgent in tone.

Do not mention collection agency or legal action at this stage. It is still possible to retain goodwill while collecting the amount owed.

SAMPLE URGENT APPEAL LETTER

March 10, 1993

Purchase, etc.

Deanne Wilson:

Your order from ABC Graphics for 20,000 flyers was delivered on January 10, 1993. Unfortunately, we have not received any payment.

Please use the enclosed self-addressed, stamped envelope to send your payment today. It is extremely important that we receive payment no later than Friday, March 15.

If you are having difficulties with the payment, contact me by that date. I will do all that I can to be of assistance. My telephone number is (676) 342-9023.

Sincerely,

COLLECT CALLS ACCEPTED.

Enc.

Step 3: The Ultimatum Letter

Your goal in the ultimatum letter is to receive payment. It is probably not possible to retain your reader's goodwill.

You can refer to a collection agency and legal action, but do not threaten your reader. Although the law is in your corner, a knowledge of the 1978 Fair Debt Collection Practice Act is important. That act is specific about what you can and cannot do in collecting a debt.

Collection agencies are available, but their services are costly.

SAMPLE ULTIMATUM LETTER

April 10,1993

Purchase, etc.

Deanne Wilson:

On January 10, 1993, ABC Graphics printed 20,000 flyers for you. The bill for that service is now three months overdue.

I do not want to submit your account to a collection agency or to follow other legal means to receive payment. Such actions are expensive and time-consuming for both of us.

However, unless I obtain payment within 10 working days from the date of this letter (Friday, April 20), you will force me into legal action.

Please use the self-addressed, stamped envelope to return your payment immediately.

Sincerely,

COLLECT CALLS ACCEPTED.

Encl.

Note. Always verify the correct amount owed, keep a copy of your correspondence, and write to the same person each time.

■ **E x e r c i s e 6 . 4**

On a separate sheet of paper, write a three-part collection series for Ms. Jones and a letter for any one of the other cases.

1. Ms. Jones bought four new tires from Gateway Tires on December 15, 1992, for a total cost of $272.12. No money was put down at the time of purchase due to a sales promotion. Write the three-part series.

2. David Fiero bought two suits from Tony's Clothes for Men November 13, 1993, for a total cost of $418.43. He returned a check for $200 on receiving your inquiry collection letter, but you have received no further payment as of January 10. Write David the urgent appeal message.

3. Huon Nguyen is a good customer of Baneda Office Supplies and Equipment (BOSE). She has bought hundreds of dollars worth of products from you over five years. Twice during that time you have had to write urgent appeal letters to her that were successful. Now she owes BOSE $676. She has not replied to your urgent appeal message. Write her an ultimatum letter, recognizing her past association with BOSE, but demanding payment.

Chapter 6 Checkpoints

✓ Try to maintain goodwill even when you deliver bad news.

✓ Remember that a person with emotions and feelings is on the receiving end of bad news.

✓ Check company policies and guidelines to become familiar with legal implications of business writing.

✓ Inquiry, appeal, and ultimatum get results.

7 | Writing for Everyone

This chapter will help you to:

- Avoid making assumptions about readers' backgrounds.
- Understand high- and low-context cultures in relation to business writing.
- Address diversity in your writing.

An American working in France as a resident engineer for an American company found that the two-hour lunch breaks—eating excellent food, cheeses, and wine at restaurants—were causing him to gain weight rapidly. He decided to take a small sack lunch to work. From then on he ate in his office while he worked.

As a result of this change, the engineer started to lose weight and went home with less work. He was pleased at so simple a solution until he received a memo from the French manager.

I sincerely hope that you are well, that your health is good, and that you are enjoying our wonderful French cooking. I have found that if I do not eat enough, I am unable to sleep, and then I get sick. I would not want that to happen to you.

The staff and I are concerned that you do not like our food, cheeses, and wines. Forgive me for noticing, but you do not eat at the restaurant with us anymore. This absence seems to mean that you do not like the staff. I must also point out that the workers are now worried that you will ask them to have shorter lunch breaks and bring a sack lunch with them to work. This will cause serious problems with the unions.

The engineer solved the problem with the help of the French manager, who contacted a doctor friend. Citing health reasons, the doctor ordered the engineer to take only a sandwich and some fruit to work. The staff was happy and strike rumors ceased. ■

Since the world's economies are increasingly interdependent, it is extremely important to avoid cultural roadblocks. To do business successfully and write for an increasingly diverse readership, we need to understand the cultures and values of other countries. Some American companies (including Coca-Cola, Dow Chemical, Hewlett-Packard, IBM, and Xerox) have successfully overcome cultural roadblocks and now more than 50 percent of their profits are from sales outside the United States.

AVOID ASSUMPTIONS

As you know from experience, all readers approach your message from a variety of cultural contexts. This will certainly affect the way you write.

English is the major language used in international business. Consequently, it might be natural to assume that your readers will understand you. You should remember, though, that there are about 2,800 languages in the world, and English is a *native* language for only about $8\frac{1}{2}$ percent of the world's population.

To make your letters and memos as clear as possible there are some practices that you should follow when writing for a diverse audience.

1. Use simple words and standard English. Slang and colloquial expressions do not translate well and may change the meaning of your sentence. Many foreign readers will have learned highly struc-

tured and grammatically correct English in which meaning relies mainly on denotation. Common expressions in America English such as "there's more where that came from"; "life is a bowl of cherries"; "knock 'em dead"; "break a leg"; and "the bases are loaded", are incomprehensible for many non-English speakers.

2. Clearly define any technical/specialty words and phrases.

3. Use visual aids to clarify information.

4. Seek advice from native speakers of the same culture as your reader.

5. Read as much as possible about your reader's culture.

6. Observe the process of how your reader communicates with you: Is it indirect or direct?

7. Be sensitive to religious, national, and other important celebrations as well as dates when government offices are closed. It is a good idea to buy an international calendar that has the dates for these events. You should be aware of what is happening in your reader's country, so you can refer to appropriate situations in your messages.

8. Be sure that the reader's full name, title, and section or department are used in the letter. Be able to pronounce your reader's name correctly in case of a call or business trip.

7

Hint

Compare the following common sayings from different cultures. What values do you feel the following sayings communicate to someone from another culture?

- Don't cry over spilled milk (American).
- Life is not a bed of roses; it has thorns in it (Pakistan).
- When three people get together, it makes a great idea (Japanese).
- The empty can makes the most noise (Malaysia).
- The mouth is a source of trouble (Japanese).
- The squeaky wheel gets oiled (American).
- If you try to work, you will succeed (Vietnamese).
- What can God do with a monkey more than make him a monkey (Jordan).
- Tell me who your friends are and I'll tell you who you are (Turkey).
- Failure is the mother of success (Hong Kong).
- There are three people walking in front of me; one can be my teacher (Chinese).

HIGH- AND LOW-CONTEXT CULTURES

When discussing communication in terms of cultural differences it is useful to divide cultures into two groups, high- and low-context, based on the relative level of explicit information that needs to accompany written or verbal communication.[1] In low-context cultures the speaker or writer needs to explicitly state information to help the receiver understand a message. In high-context cultures, there isn't a need for such explicit information—it is OK for the writer or speaker to imply information less directly.

As you can see in the following figure, as you move from low to high context, there is less of a need for exact information and more use of subtlety and nuance in language.

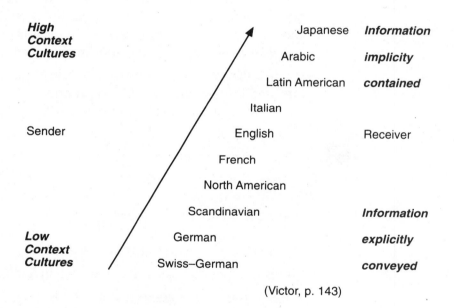

(Victor, p. 143)

Other characteristics associated with high- and low-context cultures include:

High-Context	**Low-Context**
Long-term view	Short-term view
Common knowledge and experience	Little knowledge and experience

---

[1] D. A. Victor, *International Business Communications* (New York: HarperCollins, 1992), pp. 139-146. Figure adapted with permission of HarperCollins.

High-Context	Low-Context
Implied information	Explicit information
Indirectness and vagueness tolerated	Indirectness and vagueness not tolerated
Emphasis on personal relations	Emphasis on formality, contracts
Business from friendship	Friendship from business
Feelings and moods important	Feelings and moods secondary
Confrontation is negative	Confrontation is accepted
Bad news softened	Bad news accepted
Broad goals stressed	Specific details stressed
Strong group pressure	Strong individual pressure
Power associated with person	Power associated with position
Titles are important	Titles less important
Authority seldom questioned	Authority often questioned
Unwilling to initiate action	Willing to initiate action

How does this relate to your writing style?

1. For readers in high-context cultures *how* you write a message may be more important than *what* you write. Don't be too direct. In high-context cultures, messages may begin with a paragraph that refers to the weather, the spring flowers, or an inquiry about health and family, before getting to the real point.

2. For readers in low-context cultures *what* you write is more important than *how* you write. Be more explicit and direct in your messages. In low-context cultures, messages get directly to the point, explicitly stating delivery dates, quantities ordered, and so on, rather than talking around the subject.

Practice and Review

Turn back to the memo from the French manager to the American engineer. Take a few minutes and imagine that you are the engineer. Now write a memo to the staff and workers stating why you are taking a sack lunch to work. Mention that you have no intention of changing the two-hour lunch breaks. Use an indirect approach for a higher-context culture.

_____

_____

_____

_____

_____

_____

_____

_____

DIVERSITY AT HOME

As we just discussed, business writers will increasingly need to understand cultural differences, as they write memos and letters to international business associates. In addition, keep in mind that the United States is becoming increasingly more culturally diverse. If you write memos and letters to co-workers who come from culturally diverse backgrounds, follow the guidelines on culture and context we just discussed. In addition, consider the following suggestions:

1. Use common sense and good manners. Show respect for the individual and for cultural heritage.

2. Follow up written memos and letters, if appropriate, with a personal conversation or a telephone call to ensure that your message was received correctly and understood.

3. Write important instructions in English and, if applicable, in the native language of your readers. Examples include safety directions, hazardous materials information, and deadlines for health benefit plans.

4. Promote recognition and awards that are especially important to cross-cultural understanding. Your awareness of cultural events will be appreciated by individuals and their families.

5. Be flexible, sensitive, and patient with all readers. Never use discriminatory words.

6. Check the contents and process of your message with people who represent diverse groups before sending memos and letters to cross-cultural readers. You cannot be expected to be aware of all such groups, but research will usually tell you whether you have African, Hispanic, Asian, and other minority Americans as your readers.

7. Remember, when organizing your message, that some of the groups in your audience may have ambivalent attitudes toward others. Ignoring such social realities can earn you the dislike of both groups.

8. Stick to facts, common issues, and mutual objectives. Avoid conjecture, opinion, and self-interest goals.

9. Be honest. Be yourself. It is prudent to be more formal and con-
servative if you are unsure of your audience. Some groups may be
acutely attuned to patronizing attitudes and maternal or paternal connotations from people of different cultures.

10. Be consistent. Never express your political, religious, or cultural
biases in business writing.

AVOID GROUP-BIASED LANGUAGE

Many writers try to recognize cultural diversity, but they are often unaware
of appropriate strategies and tend to make errors. Here are some tips to
help you avoid errors when you are writing to cross-cultural groups:

1. Keep your words value-neutral. A good question to ask yourself is
whether your words respect the reader's age, belief system, disability,
ethnic origin, gender, and race. A useful source is *The Dictionary of Bias
Free Usage*.[2]

2. Don't write anything that seems to give certain individuals or
groups preferential treatment.

3. Try to become knowledgable about your reader's ethnic and geo-
graphic background, so you are more aware of their concerns and
interests.

4. Use your knowledge of the individual's history discreetly.

█ **E x e r c i s e   7 . 1**

Think about the following sentences and the biased connotations they
contain. Then write a sentence that removes the bias without changing the
meaning of the sentence.

Example:

All women want to buy nutritional food for their children. (The assumption is that all women are mothers and that fathers are not concerned with
their children's diet.)

Correction: All parents want to buy nutritional food for their children.

---

[2] Rosalie Maggio, *The Dictionary of Bias Free Usage*: Oryx Press, 1991.

1. The gals in the office are very competent.

_____

2. The Chinese salesman is very effective with Asian customers.

_____

3. She's a white, South African immigrant, so I don't think that she will
   be effective teaching in an inner-city black school.

_____

_____

4. Amanda is a strict Seventh Day Adventist, and Rashad is a black
   muslim.

_____

5. I'm sure that Jill would be good at the job but she is in a wheel-
   chair; she's handicapped.

_____

_____

6. Bill and Mary are gay and lesbian, and I don't think that they would
   make good salespeople.

_____

_____

Chapter 7 Checkpoints

✓ Make sure memos and letters to nonnative English speakers are clear and straightforward—stick to standard English.

✓ Write memos and letters with attention to high- or low-context characteristics of the reader.

✓ Be aware and sensitive to cross-cultural differences—abroad and at home.

✓ Use value-neutral language and avoid group bias.

Post-Test

Test yourself on the nine chapters that you have finished by circling the best response to the following statements.

1. The phrase "the medium is the message" means that:
   a. Common sense is important when you write messages.
   b. The physical form the message takes is initially the message.
   c. The senses of sight and touch are used most by your readers.
   d. Your memos and letters build partnerships with your readers.

2. When using the indirect/informal approach, your first paragraph should:
   a. Get immediately to the main point.
   b. State the action you want.
   c. Obtain interest with a short introduction.
   d. Ask a question of your reader.

3. The best length for most business sentences is:
   a. 1–10 words.
   b. 1–15 words.
   c. 1–27 words.
   d. 1–35 words.

4. The symbolism of language is important for successful business messages because symbols:
   a. Can change the intention behind the words you choose.
   b. Convey information that is always misunderstood.
   c. Change the denotation of your words.
   d. Are too flippant and casual in tone.

5. Routine, good news, and goodwill memos and letters are the easiest of messages to write because:
   a. They require little time and organization.
   b. They aren't seen as important by your readers.
   c. They can be read quickly.
   d. None of the above.

6. In bad news messages, you should avoid:

    a. Visual and emotional clutter.

    b. Personal comments.

    c. Absolutes such as *always* and *never*.

    d. All of the above.

7. In writing the three-part collection series you should:

    a. Attempt to obtain results and be legal.

    b. Be consistent in your mailing timetable.

    c. Retain your reader's goodwill above all other objectives.

    d. *a* and *b*, but not *c*.

8. In high-context cultures, how you write your messages is often:

    a. Less important than what you write.

    b. More important than what you write.

    c. Completely ignored by the reader.

    d. None of the above.

9. The following sentence contains examples of biased words: "The women and the guys in the office are divided into management and workers, who have one boss that they see as Mr. Honcho, since he is a mafialike figure." How many biased words does the sentence contain?

    a. Two.

    b. Three.

    c. Five.

    d. Seven.

Business Skills Express Series

This growing series of books addresses a broad range of key business skills and topics to meet the needs of employees, human resource departments, and training consultants.

To obtain information about these and other Business Skills Express books, please contact the Director of Special Sales, McGraw-Hill, 11 West 19th Street, New York, NY 10011. Or contact your local bookstore.

The Participative Leader
ISBN   0-7863-0252-6

Building Customer Loyalty
ISBN   0-7863-0253-4

Getting and Staying Organized
ISBN   0-7863-0254-2

Business Etiquette
ISBN   0-7863-0273-9

Training Skills for Supervisors
ISBN   0-7863-0308-5